# School of Systematic Theology
## Book 1

### God's Throne Room:
The Doctrines of God, Christ, the Holy Spirit, and Angels

A ministry of

*Striving for Eternity Ministries*

# School of Systematic Theology
# - Book 1 -

## God's Throne Room

### The Doctrine of God

Lesson 1 - The Attributes of God, Part 1

Lesson 2 - The Attributes of God, Part 2

Lesson 3 - The Attributes of God, Part 3

Lesson 4 - The Names of God

Lesson 5 - The Triunity of God

### The Doctrine of Christ

Lesson 6 - The Deity of Christ

Lesson 7 - The Humanity of Christ, Part 1

Lesson 8 - The Humanity of Christ, Part 2

Lesson 9 - The Ministry of Christ

### The Doctrine of the Holy Spirit

Lesson 10 - The Person of the Holy Spirit

Lesson 11 - The Ministry of the Holy Spirit, Part 1

Lesson 12 - The Ministry of the Holy Spirit, Part 2

Lesson 13 - Understanding Biblical Tongues

### The Doctrine of Angels

Lesson 14 - Holy and Evil Angels

Lesson 15 - Satan

### Bibliography

*A Ministry of:*

Striving For Eternities Ministries
www.StrivingForEternity.org

# SECTION I:

## The Doctrine of God

# Lesson 1:
# The Attributes of God, Part 1

In developing an understanding of who God is, there is only one source to which we may turn: the Word of God.

Practical benefits of studying the doctrine of God:
To understand who God is will change one's life (Isaiah 6:1-8).

    Changed Isaiah's view of _____
    Changed Isaiah's view of _____
    Changed Isaiah's view of _____

    Knowing God better will enable a believer to follow His commands better (1 Peter 1:16).

To understand what the Bible says about God will help the Christian to refute various false doctrines (1 Peter 3:15).

To know God in a greater way will develop _____ in the life of the believer (Job 28:12, 23-28).

To understand all that God has revealed about who He is will equip believers to _____ Him better (Psalm 111).

Attributes are those qualities which cannot be separated from the idea of God. In other words, a discussion about God must include all His attributes. Notice several key characteristics of attributes:

    Attributes cannot grow or change.
    Attributes are what God has revealed about Himself. They are not, however, the sum total of God.
    Attributes may be ascribed to any Person of the Godhead.

God's attributes can be described as they relate to His deity, His personality, and His morality.

# I. ATTRIBUTES RELATED TO GOD'S DEITY

Attributes related to God's deity are attributes which God _____ possesses. These are true of God only.

### A. Incomprehensibility

Definition
God's nature is impossible to _____. Though man can know God, God cannot be fully known. Man needs not to know God _____, but to know Him _____.

Scriptures
Psalm 145:3
Romans 11:33-34
1 Corinthians 2:11

### B. Immutability

Definition
God's nature is incapable of _____.

Scriptures
James 1:17
Hebrews 13:8

### C. Infinity

Definition
God has no _____ or _____ outside of His nature. God is infinite in existence, time, space, knowledge, power, and presence.

Scriptures
Job 11:7-9
Psalm 145:3
Romans 11:33

### D. Self-Existence

Definition
God is infinite in _____. God's existence is not dependent upon anything _____ of Himself.

Scriptures
- Deuteronomy 32:40
- Isaiah 43:10

### E. Eternality

Definition
God is infinite in _____. He has and will continue to exist _____.

Scriptures
- Psalm 90:2
- Revelation 1:8

### F. Immensity

Definition
God is infinite in _____. God is not limited to space.

Scriptures
- Psalm 113:4-6

### G. Omniscience

Definition
God is all-knowing. He knows all things past, present, future, real, and possible.

Scriptures
- 1 John 3:20
- Hebrews 4:13
- Matthew 11:21

### H. Omnipotence

Definition
God is all-powerful, able to do anything _____ with His nature. God does all that He wills to do; He does not do all He is capable of doing.

Scriptures
> Mark 14:36
> Revelation 19:6

## I. Omnipresence

Definition
> God in His _____ is in all places all the time.

Scriptures
> Jeremiah 23:24

## J. Sovereignty

Definition
> This is in reference to His _____ power and His position as the chief being in the entire universe.

Scriptures
> Ephesians 1:11, 2:10
> Psalms 115:3, 135:6

## THOUGHT QUESTIONS FOR LESSON 1

1) A Christian says to you that knowing doctrine is not that important because it is not practical. How would you respond to him?

2) Is it possible to hide our sins from God? Which attribute would you cite to support your answer?

3) A coworker tells you that he overheard your discussion with another believer about the Second Coming of Christ. He then asserts that because so many things about religion change, religion is not trustworthy. Which attribute of God would be a comfort to this person?

4) A Jehovah's Witness insists to you that the trinity cannot be possible because it does not make any sense. Which verses would you use to explain how the attributes of God support this doctrine?

5) A Christian friend shares with you that he is battling loneliness in his life. What advice would you offer him? Explain how remembering the attributes of God comforts a lonely believer.

# Lesson 2:
# The Attributes of God, Part 2

Attributes are those qualities which cannot be separated from the idea of God. In other words, a discussion about God must include all His attributes. Notice several key characteristics of attributes:

Attributes cannot grow or change.
Attributes are what God has revealed about Himself. They are not, however, the sum total of God.
Attributes may be ascribed to any Person of the Godhead.

God's attributes can be described as they relate to His deity, His personality, and His morality.

## I. ATTRIBUTES RELATED TO GOD'S DEITY
## II. ATTRIBUTES RELATED TO GOD'S PERSONALITY

These qualities, which are based on the Personhood of God, make up the _____ of God in man (Genesis 1:26).

### A. Spirituality

Definition
The essence of God is Spirit. This is the invisible source of personality.

Scriptures
Zechariah 4:6
John 4:24

**Questions:** If God is Spirit, how do we explain all the passages that speak of people seeing God? These are called _____.

If God is Spirit, what about those passages which speak of Him having feet, hands, eyes, ears, etc.? These are called _____.

## B. Life

Definition
God is living in that He possesses within Himself the source of all being and activity.

Scriptures
Joshua 3:10
Psalm 84:2
1 Timothy 3:15

## C. Self-Consciousness

Definition
God is aware of His own existence. He knows Himself _____.

Scriptures
1 Corinthians 2:11
Isaiah 45:5

**NOTE:** While the first three attributes of God's personality describe His personality as a whole, the following three describe the elements that make up His personality.

## D. Emotion

Definition
God is capable of expressing emotion. Emotion arises from and is necessary to _____.

Scriptures
Look up the following verses, and name the emotions of God found in them:

John 3:16 _____
Psalm 145:8 _____
Genesis 6:6 _____
Proverbs 6:16-19 _____
1 Peter 5:6-7 _____
Deuteronomy 6:15 _____
Psalm 5:4-5 _____

## E. Intelligence

Definition:
Knowledge - the perception of facts as they _____.

Understanding - insight into the _____ of facts.

Wisdom – the ability to place facts in the proper relationship to one another and use toward a good end.

## F. Self-Determination (Will, Purpose)

Definition
God's activity is determined by Him alone. He is a purposive being.

Scriptures
Job 23:13
Three aspects of God's personality working together:

_____
_____
_____

Genesis 1, 2
God's self-determination seen in _____

Ephesians 1:3-13
God's self-determination seen in His plan of _____

Romans 8:29-30
God's self-determination seen in His plan for the _____

## THOUGHT QUESTIONS FOR LESSON 2

1. A Catholic friend admits to you his frustration with the futility of praying to the various idols his church venerates. Which of God's attributes will help him to distinguish idols from the true God?

2. A friend grieving the loss of a loved one remarks that God cannot possibly understand her feelings because He is not a man. What attributes of God could you use to comfort your friend?

3. Someone tells you that God is going to give him a car because he had told God that he needed one, and, therefore, God is obligated to provide one. Which attributes of God has this person overlooked?

4. A Latter Day Saint (or Mormon) concludes that all the verses referencing God's hands, feet, etc. mean that God has a body. How would you answer this person?

5. What is the basis for our worship, and how does this apply to our life? See John 4:24.

# Lesson 3:
# The Attributes of God, Part 3

Attributes are those qualities which cannot be separated from the idea of God. In other words, a discussion about God must include all His attributes. Notice several key characteristics of attributes:

> Attributes cannot grow or change.
> Attributes are what God has revealed about Himself. They are not, however, the sum total of God.
> Attributes may be ascribed to any Person of the Godhead.

God's attributes can be described as they relate to His deity, His personality, and His morality.

## I. ATTRIBUTES RELATED TO GOD'S DEITY
## II. ATTRIBUTES RELATED TO GOD'S PERSONALITY
## III. ATTRIBUTE RELATED TO GOD'S MORALITY

These are qualities of the divine essence and have to do with the moral realm. This is first within Himself and then in how He relates His morality to His created beings.

### A. Holiness

Explanation
  Negatively
  God is _____ from all forms of uncleanness and evil.
  (Leviticus 11:44, 20:26)

  Positively
  God is _____.
  (1 John 1:5)

Expressions
  Righteousness
    Definition
      God demands that all moral beings _____ to His moral perfection.

    Scriptures
      Leviticus 11:44-45
      1 Peter 1:16

Justice
> Definition
>> God judges _____ non-conformity to His moral perfections.
>
> Scriptures
>> Deuteronomy 32:4
>> Psalm 7:11
>> Romans 2:2

Goodness
> Definition
>> God is perfectly _____, doing that which is right and good.
>
> Scriptures
>> Psalm 119:68, 145:9

Wrath
> Definition
>> God will give _____ for an offense or a crime.
>
> Scriptures
>> Exodus 22:22-24
>> Romans 4:15

## B. Truth

Explanation
> God's knowledge, declaration and representation eternally conform to _____.
> (John 17:3)

Expressions
> Veracity
>> Definition
>> God does not _____ on truth.
>>
>> Scriptures
>>> Numbers 23:19
>>> Titus 1:2

Faithfulness
- Definition
  - God _____ all His promises.

- Scriptures
  - 1 Peter 4:19
  - Hebrews 10:23

## C. Love

Explanation
This is that which moves God to give of Himself.
(John 3:16, 1 John 4:8)

Expressions
- Grace
  - Definition
    - God's love expressed in _____ to man that which was not deserved.
  - Scriptures
    - Titus 2:11-14
    - Ephesians 1:6-7

- Mercy
  - Definition
    - God's love expressed in the _____ of that which is deserved
  - Scriptures
    - Romans 6:23
    - Ephesians 2:4-5

- Longsuffering
  - Definition
    - God's love expressed in the _____ of the stubborn wills of mankind
  - Scriptures
    - 2 Peter 3:9

## THOUGHT QUESTIONS FOR LESSON 3

1. An unsaved friend states that he believes that because God is a God of love, He could never send anyone to a literal hell. How would you answer him?

2. A Christian friend tells you that the most important thing about God is His love. What would be your reply?

3. If God's holiness means that He separates Himself from all that is evil and unclean, which of His other attributes will allow sinful men who believe in Christ to dwell with Him?

4. Your neighbor who knows you are a Christian shares her doubt that Jesus Christ will come again. How would you reassure her that He will?

5. A brother in Christ confides in you that his life is being dominated by sin, and he feels that God cannot love him anymore. What could you share with this person?

# Lesson 4: The Names of God

The names of God give us further evidence of His essence and character. In his book *The Names of God*, Nathan Stone notes, "... a name in the Old Testament was often an indication of a person's character or of some peculiar quality. But what one name could be adequate to describe God's greatness?"

The "name of God" is His self-revelation to man.

This lesson will focus on the primary names for God in the Old Testament. New Testament names for God will be discussed in the lessons on the Triunity of God, the deity of Christ, and the deity of the Holy Spirit.

## I. *EL (ELOHIM)*

### A. Meaning

The name means _____ or _____.

The word is often used in the plural to identify the _____ of God and allows for the teaching of the _____.

This name of God focuses on His attribute of _____.

### B. Compounds

*El Elyon*
    Translation _____
    (Genesis 14:18-20)

*El Shaddai*
    Translation _____

    It highlights God's _____.
    (Genesis 17:1, 28:3)

*El Olam*
    Translation _____

    It highlights God's _____.
    (Genesis 21:33)

*El Roi*
    Translation _____

    It highlights God's _____.
    (Genesis 16:13)

**C. Usage** - Over 2500 times

**D. Translation** - Usually translated "God"

## II. *YHWH* or *JEHOVAH*

### A. Meaning
The name means _____ and is used in reference to God's _____ relationships.

It comes from the Hebrew verb *"to be."*
(Exodus 3:14)

It is first used in Genesis 2:4.

### B. Compounds

*YHWH Jireh*
    Translation _____
    (Genesis 22:14)

*YHWH Rapha*
    Translation _____
    (Exodus 15:26)

*YHWH Nissi*
    Translation _____
    (Exodus 17:15)

*YHWH Mekaddeschem*
    Translation _____
    (Exodus 31:13)

*YHWH Shalom*
    Translation _____
    (Judges 6:24)

*YHWH Sabbaoth*
　　Translation _____
　　(1 Samuel 1:3, Isaiah 6:5)

*YHWH Roi*
　　Translation _____
　　(Psalm 23:1)

*YHWH Tsidkenu*
　　Translation _____
　　(Jeremiah 23:6)

*YHWH Shammah*
　　Translation _____
　　(Ezekiel 48:35)

**C. Usage** - Approximately 6800 times

**D. Translation** – "LORD" or "GOD" (all upper case letters)

## III. *ADONAI*

### A. Meaning

　　Translation _____ or
　　_____

　　When used of God, it is a reference to His _____ and
　　_____.
　　(Isaiah 6:8, Exodus 4:10-12)

**B. Usage** - Approximately 300 times (used of men, etc.)

**C. Translation** – "Lord"

## THOUGHT QUESTIONS FOR LESSON 4

1. Read Psalm 19. Write down the names of God found in the text. How are the names related to the works of God mentioned?

2. A Jehovah's Witness says to you that there is only one God and that nowhere in the Old Testament do we see a hint of the Trinity. What name(s) of God might you share with him? What insight would you share?

3. A Christian friend is worrying because she thinks she may lose her place to live and has no way to provide for herself. What name of God would comfort her?

4. What implications on our personal lives does the name *Adonai* have?

# Lesson 5:
# The Triunity of God

Though the terms *Trinity, Triunity,* or *Trinitarian* are not found in Scripture, we use them to describe God as one in essence yet existing in three personalities. The Triunity refers to the doctrine of the _____ Persons in _____ God.

This section will survey the Triunity of God as found in the Old and New Testaments. Further discussion of the Trinity will be presented in the lessons on the deity of Christ and the deity of the Holy Spirit.

## I. THE TRINITY IN THE OLD TESTAMENT

The Old Testament emphasis is clearly the uniqueness and unity of God. This foundation in understanding God was necessary in order to refute the primary religious deviation at the time, _____.

However, even though the Old Testament emphasizes the unity of God, we still see hints to the truth of the Triunity.

### A. The Use of _____

Significance
*Elohim*, a plural noun, is used with singular verbs to describe the one true God. This name demonstrates that the unity of God is not contradictory to the Triunity of God.

Scriptures
Genesis 1:1

### B. The Work of the _____ of God

Significance
In the above verse, we witness the Spirit of God involved in creation.

Scriptures
Genesis 1:2

### C. The Use of _____

Significance
The use of plural pronouns in describing the one true God again hint at the teaching of multiple Persons within the Godhead.

Scriptures
> Genesis 1:26, 3:22
> Isaiah 6:8

### D. The Use of _____

Significance
> Many who oppose the doctrine of the Triunity claim that it contradicts the doctrine of only one God. The word used in Deuteronomy 6:4 which is translated as "one" (*echad*), does not refer to oneness in the sense of _____, but oneness in the sense _____.

Scriptures
> Deuteronomy 6:4

### E. The Appearance of the _____

Significance
> These and other Christophanies (Theophanies) are able to exist both in heaven and in one place in time to accept worship.

Scriptures
> Genesis 16:9-11, 31:11-13
> Exodus 3:2-5

### F. The Prophecies of the _____

Significance
> In the variety of passages prophesying the coming Messiah, He is spoken of as being a distinct Person the same in essence as God.

Scriptures
> Isaiah 7:14, 9:6, 40:3
> Psalm 45:6-7

## II. THE TRINITY IN THE NEW TESTAMENT

While the Old Testament emphasized the _____ of God and at the time allowed for the teaching of the Triunity, the New Testament clearly presents the Godhead as one in essence, yet existing in three Persons.

**A. Three Persons are recognized as _____.**

The Father is recognized as God.
(John 16:27)

The Son is recognized as God.
(John 1:1, 8:58, 20:26-9)

The Spirit is recognized as God.
(Acts 5:3-4)

All three Persons are seen in conjunction with each other.
(Matthew 28:19, 2 Corinthians 13:4, Titus 3:4-7, 1 Peter 1:2)

**B. Three are one in _____.**

The Father is one with the Son.
(John 1:1; 10:30; 14:8-9, 23)

The Spirit is one with the Son.
(John 16:13-15, Romans 8:8-11)

The Spirit is one with the Father.
(Acts 5:3-4, Romans 8:8-11)

**C. Three are _____ from each other.**

Distinction in _____ does not mean there is distinction in essence.

The Father is distinct from the Son.
(John 14:28 [c.f. Philippians 2:5-8], Galatians 4:4)

The Spirit is distinct from the Father and the Son.
(John 14:16-17)

These three Persons of the Godhead, each and all divine, are to be recognized as _____ in _____, equally existing in three _____.

**NOTE:** Many who deny the Trinity do so because they cannot explain it from a human perspective, but there are *many* things about God that are completely beyond our comprehension (i.e. how He hears and answers all prayer; is everywhere at the same time; knows all things past, present, future, and possible in one present reality). No human can explain these things. However, because the Bible teaches the reality of the Triunity of God, we believe it though we cannot explain it.

## THOUGHT QUESTIONS FOR LESSON 5

1. A Jewish friend of yours discusses the difficulty he has accepting that Christ is God and that the Old Testament teaches that there is only one God. How would you help him with his difficulty?

2. A Jehovah's Witness admits that the Angel of Jehovah must have been an appearing of the pre-incarnate Christ. What truth would you share with him to illustrate this?

3. A Jehovah's Witness tells you that nowhere in the Old Testament is Christ suggested to be God. What text(s) would you offer him? What would you emphasize?

4. Another Jehovah's Witness cites John 14:28 to indicate that Christ could not have been God. How would you respond?

# SECTION II:

# The Doctrine of Christ

# Lesson 6:
# The Deity of Christ

Christians who have contact with any of the major cults (Jehovah's Witnesses, Mormons, The Way International, World Wide Church of God, etc.) or world religions (Islam, Judaism, etc.) have experienced the need to convince these people of the deity of Christ. In this study we will see three indications of the deity of Christ: the names, the works, and the attributes.

## I. THE NAMES OF CHRIST INDICATE HIS DEITY.

### A. In the Old Testament

Mighty God
(Isaiah 9:6)

Lord
(Psalm 110:1)

*YHWH*
(Jeremiah 23:6, Isaiah 40:3)

Everlasting Father
(Isaiah 9:6)

Immanuel
(Isaiah 7:14, cf. Matthew 1:23)

### B. In the New Testament

God
(John 1:1, 20:24-29; 1 Timothy 1:1, 4:10; Titus 1:3-4; 2:10, 13; 3:4, 6)

Lord
    Used by _____
    (Luke 6:46, Mark 2:23-28)

    Used by _____
        The disciples
        (Luke 6:46, John 13:13)

        Mary Magdalene and Mary
        (Luke 24:34)

        Peter
        (Acts 10:36)

        Paul
        (Acts 26:15)

        John
        (Revelation 19:16)

**NOTE:** Some would deny that this title is a reference of deity because it may be used to refer to a man. While this is true, it is obviously used in reference to deity, as well. The context determines the usage. These references are clear statements of the deity of Christ.

Son of God

    Significance
        The word *son*, while it can mean _____, most often is used to refer to one who partakes of or is _____ with the one to whom he is son.

        Some examples are:
        Sons of thunder
        (Mark 3:17)

        Son of perdition
        (John 17:12; 2 Thessalonians 2:3)

        Son of encouragement
        (Acts 4:36)

        Also, note that Christ's sonship is always connected to His incarnation.

    Scriptures
        Matthew 16:16
        Mark 1:11, 5:7, 15:39
        John 10:31-39

The Word

    Significance
        To the Hebrew, the idea of the Word is that _____.
        Thus, the Lord Jesus Christ is considered the full communication of God to man.

    Scriptures
        John 1:1, 14
        Revelation 19:13

First and Last

> Significance
>> The Lord Jesus Christ, in His revelation to John, used over and over again a title ascribed to _____ in the Old Testament.
>
> Scriptures
>> Isaiah 44:6, 48:12
>> Revelation 1:11, 17; 2:8; 22:13

*I AM*

> Significance
>> This is a statement of deity. It emphasizes the pre-existence and eternality of Jesus.
>
> Scriptures
>> Exodus 3:14
>> cf. John 8:58-59

Savior

> Significance
>> *YHWH* in the Old Testament was known as the only Savior, yet this title was given to _____.
>
> Scriptures
>> Isaiah 43:11, 45:21
>> Hosea 13:4
>> Luke 1:47
>> Titus 1:3-4, 3:4-6

## II. THE WORKS OF CHRIST INDICATE HIS DEITY.

### A. Creation
(John 1:3, 1 Corinthians 8:6, Ephesians 3:9, Colossians 1:16, Hebrews 1:2)

### B. Forgiveness of Sins
(Matthew 9:2-6, Mark 2:7)

## C. Giving of Life

_____ Life
(John 11:17, 37-44)

_____ Life
(John 10:28)

## D. Acceptance of Worship

By accepting worship, He could not be...
   A mere man
   (John 10:33)

   An angel
   (Colossians 2:18, Revelation 19:10, 22:8-9)

By accepting worship, He *must* be God.
   Matthew 14:33
   Luke 24:51-52
   Philippians 2:9-11

## E. Judgment of Mankind
(John 5:22, 27; Acts 10:42; 2 Timothy 4:1)

# III. THE ATTRIBUTES OF CHRIST INDICATE HIS DEITY.

## A. Incomprehensibility
(Ephesians 3:8, 19)

## B. Sovereignty
(Romans 14:10-12)

## C. Omniscience
(John 2:24-25, 16:30-32)

## D. Omnipotence
(John 5:19, 21, Colossians 1:17)

## E. Omnipresence
(Matthew 28:20, Hebrews 4:13)

## F. Immutability
(Hebrews 13:8)

## G. Eternality
(John 1:1, 8:58; Revelation 1:8)

## H. Holiness
(Mark 1:24)

Finally, Colossians 2:9 ascribes to Christ one of the greatest statements of deity in Scripture: "For in Him dwelleth all the fullness of the Godhead bodily."

After examining the totality of information on the deity of Christ, one must say He is one of three things:

_____ – That is, He deceived those who followed Him, telling them He was God.

_____ – That is, He was so deluded He did not know what He was saying, claiming to be God.

_____ – **He is who He says He is: the King of Kings and the Lord of Lords.**

ASSIGNMENT: Study, and commit to memory the necessary verses which demonstrate the deity of Christ.

# Lesson 7:
# The Humanity of Christ, Part 1

Many are confused when they consider that Jesus is both fully _____ and fully _____. While the deity of Christ is widely debated, His humanity currently seems to be accepted as fact.

This lesson will focus on Christ and the importance of His humanity, His existence before humanity, and His entrance into humanity, all three of which are often misunderstood.

## I. IMPORTANCE OF CHRIST'S HUMANITY

### A. Concerning His _____

Jesus' life as a man provided the pattern for all men to follow.
(1 Peter 2:21)

### B. Concerning His Everlasting _____

Only a Man can faithfully represent men to God.
(Hebrews 2:17-18)

### C. Concerning His Daily Provision of _____

He understands our lives because He lived His own. Coming to Him, we "obtain mercy and find grace to help in time of need."
(Hebrews 2:17-18, 4:15-16)

## II. CHRIST AND HIS EXISTENCE BEFORE HUMANITY

### A. False Statements about Christ's Preexistence

Christ was merely a _____.

Christ was an _____.

## B. Correct Statement about Christ's Preexistence

Christ existed prior to His _____ into humanity. (John 8:56-59). From the previous lesson, we recognize that He existed not as an angel, but as _____.

# III. CHRIST AND HIS ENTRANCE INTO HUMANITY

His entrance into humanity is called the _____. We will note the preparation, the process, and the purpose for His entrance into humanity.

## A. The Preparation for His Entrance into Humanity

Prophecies of the Old Testament
Genesis 3:15
Isaiah 7:14, 9:6, 42:1-4, 53:1ff, 61:1-2
Micah 5:2-3

Ministry of a Forerunner
The Old Testament Promise
Isaiah 40:3
Malachi 3:1, 4:5

The New Testament Fulfillment
Matthew 3:1-12
cf. 2 Kings 1:8 — "So they answered him, 'A hairy man wearing a leather belt around his waist.' And he said, 'It is Elijah the Tishbite.'"
Luke 1:17

**PROBLEM:** Some see a contradiction here because John the Baptist answered that he was not Elijah (John 1:21) while Christ said that John was the forerunner (Matthew 11:14, 17:11-13).

**SOLUTION:** John was one like Elijah was (Luke 1:17). In order for Christ to present the kingdom to the Jews sincerely, there needed to be a forerunner like Elijah. John fulfilled that role. When asked whether he was Elijah, he rejected that he was a resurrected Elijah.

## B. The Process of His Entry into Humanity

Isaiah 7:14, Matthew 1:21-23
These texts emphasize the _____ by which Christ was to enter into humanity, namely the virgin birth and conception of the Holy Spirit.

John 1:1-14
> This passage explains the _____ that the Word, which was eternal and coexisting with God while possessing the same essence (1:1), became the God-Man.

Philippians 2:5-8
> These verses focus on the _____ of Christ: He "voluntarily surrendered the use of His divine attributes and placed Himself under the authority and will of the Father."

## C. The Purpose of His Entrance into Humanity

These will be further considered in the studies on the ministry of Jesus Christ and the doctrine of salvation.

To provide a _____ for _____
(2 Corinthians 5:21)

To be an _____ for believers
(Philippians 2:5)

To reveal _____ to _____
(John 1:18)

To establish a _____ between God and man
(1 Timothy 2:5; 1 John 2:1-2)

To be a _____ High Priest
(Hebrews 4:14-15)

## THOUGHT QUESTIONS FOR LESSON 7

1. What is the importance of Christ's humanity?

2. What are at least three of the unique features of Christ's existence?

3. A frustrated individual who is troubled by trials and temptation says, "Christ could never understand what I'm going through!" How would you help him?

4. Could Christ sin? Why or why not?

5. Without looking back, see if you can recall the purposes for Christ entering into humanity. There are five.

   1)                          4)

   2)                          5)

   3)

6. While most accept the humanity of Christ, what would present to them a problem in connection with His humanity?

7. A skeptic produces for you what he sees as a contradiction concerning John the Baptist being Elijah. How would you answer the skeptic?

# Lesson 8:
# The Humanity of Christ, Part 2

As we covered earlier, while the deity of Christ is widely debated, His humanity currently seems to be accepted as fact. His preexistence, His entrance into humanity, and His exaltation after humanity are often misunderstood.

The previous lesson focused on Christ and the importance of His humanity, His existence before humanity, and His entrance into humanity. This lesson will focus on the evidence for Christ's humanity and His exaltation after humanity.

## I. CHRIST AND THE EVIDENCE OF HIS HUMANITY

There are at least three ways in which Christ's humanity was evidenced. Again, this is typically not debated, but it is still significant.

**A. He possessed the _____ of humanity.**

    A physical body      An immaterial soul
    (John 1:14, Hebrews 2:14)      (Matthew 28:6, Luke 23:46)

**B. He possessed the _____ of humanity.**

    Son of Man      Man
    (Luke 19:10)      (John 8:40, 1 Timothy 2:5)

**C. He possessed the _____ of humanity.**

    Emotions
        Anger      Compassion
        (Mark 3:5)      (John 13:23)

        Sorrow      Fear
        (John 11:35)      (John 12:27)

    Limitations
        Hunger      Thirst
        (Matthew 4:2)      (John 19:28)

        Time      Fatigue
        (Mark 11:13)      (John 4:6)

www.StrivingForEternity.org

Exhaustion		Death
(Luke 22:43)		(John 19:30)

**Question:** Since Christ possessed the fullness of humanity, was He able not to sin, or was He not able to sin?

**Answer:** Christ was not able to sin. The union of deity and humanity is a complete union in which neither nature loses something to the other. Both natures retain their attributes while functioning together in Christ.

## II. CHRIST AND HIS EXALTATION AFTER HUMANITY

Christ's exaltation consisted of five very significant events in Christian history: His crucifixion, resurrection, ascension, mediation, and revelation.

### A. His Crucifixion

Purpose
The crucifixion of Christ was accomplished voluntarily and _____ by the second Person of the Godhead for the substitutionary atonement of the sins of the human race. This will be covered in detail in the doctrine of soteriology (salvation).

Picture
Christ was introduced by John as the "Lamb of God" (John 1:29). Throughout the Old Testament, the sacrificial system pictures the future and complete work of Christ as the bloody, slain sacrifice that satisfies the wrath of God concerning the sings of men— if men receive this offering individually.

### B. His Resurrection

Foretelling of the resurrection
    In the Old Testament
        Acts 2:27 (Psalm 16:10)
        Matthew 12:38-40 (Jonah 1:17)

    By Christ
        John 2:19, 21

Fact of the resurrection
    Evidenced in Scriptural testimony
    (1 Corinthians 15)

Evidenced by eyewitness testimony

| | |
|---|---|
| Mary Magdalene (Matthew 28:8-10) | Peter (Luke 24:34) |
| Disciples on Emmaus Road (Mark 16:12) | Disciples in the upper room (Luke 24:36-43) |
| Disciples at the Sea of Galilee (John 21:1-24) | Apostles and the 500 (1 Corinthians 15:6-7) |
| Witnesses of the ascension (Acts 1:3-12) | |

Fallacies about the resurrection
The _____ Theory
A myth of the resurrection was spread through treachery or error.

The _____ Theory
Christ did not die. He passed out, but the cool air in the tomb revived Him.

The _____ Theory
Disciples were so anxious for His resurrection to take place that they saw things that did not happen. It was mass hallucination.

## C. His Ascension

Anticipation of the ascension
(Matthew 24:30, 26:64; Mark 13:26, 14:62; Luke 21:27; John 6:62)

Account of the ascension
(Acts 1:6-12)

Notice four facts concerning the ascension:

It was _____.

It was _____.

It was _____.

It was into the clouds.

## D. His Mediation

This is Christ's present ministry at the right hand of the Father, following the ascension and preceding His revelation. He is our Mediator (1 Timothy 2:5).

This aspect of Christ's ministry will be considered in the section on Christology (the ministry of Christ).

## E. His Revelation

This is the second coming of Christ from heaven. The lesson on eschatology will deal with this aspect of Christ's exaltation in depth.

## THOUGHT QUESTIONS FOR LESSON 8

1. What are three evidences of Jesus Christ's humanity?

2. A Jewish friend states that the Jewish Messiah could not have been Jesus Christ because the Jewish Messiah was not predicted to be crucified or resurrected. He believes that it is something that the Christians made up. How would you answer this friend?

3. What are some ways to show the evidence of the resurrection of Jesus Christ?

4. What are the false theories of Christ's resurrection, and how would you rebut them?

# Lesson 9:
# The Ministry of Christ

After examining the person of Jesus Christ through His deity and His humanity, it will be a great encouragement to study the ministries of Christ. We see His ministry in the three-fold, Old Testament picture of Prophet, Priest, and King.

## I. CHRIST AS PROPHET (PAST)

When we discuss Christ's ministry as a Prophet, we are talking about His work of revealing _____ to _____.

### A. Designated As a Prophet in the Old Testament

Moses in _____ predicted that God would raise up a Prophet for Israel. Luke, under the inspiration of the Holy Spirit and confirmed by Peter, recorded that the fulfillment of this was Christ _____.

### B. Declared As a Prophet in the New Testament

Christ declared Himself a Prophet.
(Luke 13:33)

Others declared Him a Prophet.

_____
(Matthew 21:11,46; Luke 7:16)

_____
(Luke 24:19)

_____
(John 4:19)

His works declared Him a Prophet.
He _____.
(Matthew 24, 25)
Definition: to tell ahead of time

He _____.
(Matthew 5-7; 23)
Definition: to proclaim the past boldly

## II. CHRIST AS PRIEST (PRESENT)

When we discuss the priestly ministry of Christ, we are talking about His present ministry of _____. As a Prophet, He speaks on behalf of God to man. As a Priest, He speaks on behalf of man to God.

### A. The Practice of the High Priest
(Leviticus 16)

He had _____ to God.

He _____ on behalf of the people.

### B. The Picture of the High Priest

The priesthood, instituted through Aaron and illustrated through Melchizedek, clearly pictured the future ministry of Christ as Priest.
(Hebrews 3, 4, 7:3)

### C. The Presence of a Great High Priest

Hebrews emphasizes the priestly ministry of Christ, many times declaring Him the "Great High Priest."
(Hebrews 4:14, 5:1-10, 7:26, 8:1, 10:12)

## III. CHRIST AS KING (PRESENT & FUTURE)

When we discuss the ministry of Christ as King, we learn the reality of His dominion and authority, or His _____.

### A. In the Old Testament

The Messiah was always presented as one who would rule His people.
(Isaiah 9:6, Daniel 7:13-14)

### B. In the New Testament

Christ as King at His First Coming
The _____ of Christ as King

Christ came to offer the kingdom and Himself as King to the Jews during His earthly ministry.
(Matthew 2:1-6, Luke 19:38-40, John 1:48-50)

The _____ of Christ as King
Because Israel rejected Christ, He held off His physical reign as King of His kingdom.

The _____ of Christ as King
There is a present realm in which Christ is King, the subjects are believers, and people enter this kingdom by means of the new birth.

Christ as King at His Second Coming
The physical reign of Christ as King will be fulfilled literally, physically, and eternally during the millennium and into eternity.
(Revelation 20:6)

## THOUGHT QUESTIONS FOR LESSON 9

1. Write down the two ministries of a prophet. Give an example of how Christ fulfilled each.

    1)

    2)

2. What is the primary difference between Christ as Prophet as Christ as Priest?

3. Does Christ function as Priest today? If He does, in what way?

4. A professing believer tells you that he has received Christ as Savior but is not ready to make Him the ruler of his life. What would you share with this person from our lesson?

# SECTION III:

# The Doctrine of the Holy Spirit

# Lesson 10:
# The Person of the Holy Spirit

In a study on the Person of the Holy Spirit, we will be looking at Scriptures that teach us about His personality and His deity. We will also examine some of the names for the Holy Spirit.

## I. HIS PERSONALITY

The personality of the Holy Spirit has been attacked since early in church history. Arius, an early heretic, denied both the eternality of Christ and the personality of the Holy Spirit (AD 320). Jehovah's Witnesses adopt the same approach used by Arius when, concerning the Holy Spirit, they state, "The Holy Spirit is God's active force...There is no basis for concluding he [sic] is a person [sic]" (*Watchtower*, 1/1/53, p.24).

There are four basic proofs of the personality of the Holy Spirit.

**A. He possesses the _____ of a Person.**

    He has an _____.
    (1 Corinthians 2:10-13)

    He has _____.
        Grief                   Love
        (Ephesians 4:30)      (Romans 15:30)

    He has a _____.
        Demonstrated in His distribution of gifts
        (1 Corinthians 12:11)

        Demonstrated in His division of servants
        (Acts 16:6-11)

**B. He performs the _____ of a Person.**

| | | |
|---|---|---|
| He teaches. (John 14:26) | He bears witness. (John 15:26) | He convicts. (John 16:7-8) |
| He gives glory. (John 16:14) | He commands. (Acts 8:29) | He calls out for service. (Acts 13:2, 4) |
| He examines. (Acts 15:28) | He leads. (Romans 8:14) | He speaks. (Revelation 2:7, 11, 17, 29; 3:6, 13, 22) |

**C. He possesses the _____ of a Person.**

The Greek word for *spirit* is a _____ word. If the authors of Scripture were to follow the normal rules of grammar, they would replace *spirit* with the pronoun_____.

John 16:13 offers an example of the _____ pronoun (i.e. "He") referring to the Holy Spirit.

**D. He receives the _____ of a Person.**

| He can be lied to. | He can be tested. | He can be resisted. |
| (Acts 5:3) | (Acts 5:9) | (Acts 7:51) |

| He can be grieved. | He can be insulted. |
| (Ephesians 4:30) | (Hebrews 10:29) |

## II. HIS DEITY

Various groups have also disputed the deity of the Holy Spirit. An example is the Jehovah's Witnesses explanation of the Spirit: "God's holy spirit [sic] is not a God, not a member of the trinity, not coequal, and is not even a person [sic]" (*Watchtower*, 7/15/57, p.432).

By observing some of the attributes used to describe the Spirit, His activities, and His association with God, we will see that the Spirit is, in fact, coequal and God in essence.

**A. His _____ of Deity**

| Omniscience | Omnipotence |
| (John 16:13, 1 Corinthians 2:10-11) | (Romans 15:19) |

| Omnipresence | Eternality |
| (Psalm 139:7) | (Hebrews 9:14) |

| Holiness | Truth |
| (Luke 11:13) | (1 John 5:6) |

**B. His _____ of Deity**

| Creation | Inspiration |
| (Genesis 1:2, Psalm 104:30) | (2 Peter 1:21) |

Regeneration ,
(Titus 3:5, Ephesians 1:13, 2 Thessalonians 2:13, 1 Peter 1:2)

**C. His _____ of Deity**

Associated with _____
(Acts 28:25-27, cf. Isaiah 6:8-10; Hebrews 10:15-17, cf. Jeremiah 31:31-34)

Associated with _____
(Acts 5:1-4, 1 Corinthians 3:16, Matthew 12:31)

Associated with the _____
(Matthew 28:19, 2 Corinthians 13:14, 1 Corinthians 12:4-6, 1 Peter 1:2)

Associated with _____
(John 14:16-17)

## III. HIS IDENTITY

**A. Described in the _____ of the Holy Spirit**

By observing some of the illustrations used to describe the Spirit of God, we may also see some of His _____.

| | |
|---|---|
| Clothing (Luke 24:49) | Dove (Matthew 3:16) |
| Earnestness (2 Corinthians 1:22, 5:5) | Seal (Ephesians 1:13, 2 Corinthians 1:22) |
| Water (John 7:38-39) | Wind (John 3:8) |

**B. Described in the _____ of the Holy Spirit**

| | |
|---|---|
| Spirit of Grace (Hebrews 10:29) | Spirit of Glory (1 Peter 4:12-19) |
| Spirit of the Living God (2 Corinthians 3:3) | Spirit of Christ (Romans 8:9) |
| Spirit of Truth (John 14:17) | Spirit of Life (Romans 8:2) |
| Comforter (John 14:26) | |

## THOUGHT QUESTIONS FOR LESSON 10

1. A Jehovah's Witness explains to you that the Holy Spirit is only a force coming out of Jehovah and is not even a Person. What are the four general proofs of His personality that you would use to answer this individual?

    1)

    2)

    3)

    4)

2. The same Jehovah's Witness claims that the Holy Spirit is not God. Give some verses that associate the Holy Spirit with God.

3. How can understanding the Holy Spirit as a Person be beneficial for the believer's life?

# Lesson 11:
# The Ministry of the Holy Spirit, Part 1

The ministry of the Holy Spirit in the lives of men throughout the ages is a vital study for today. Many groups either de-emphasize or exaggerate what the ministry of the Spirit is. Once again, our understanding of this doctrine must come through a study of all the Scriptures.

This lesson will examine the ministry of the Spirit in the Old Testament, during the life of Christ, and in the future.

## I. THE MINISTRY OF THE SPIRIT IN THE OLD TESTAMENT

We see the Spirit of God ministering in basically four different circumstances.

### A. Creation

The Spirit was active in the creation of the _____.
(Genesis 1:2)

The Spirit is active in the creation of _____.
(Job 33:4)

### B. Restraint
(Genesis 6:3, 1 Peter 3:20)

### C. Revelation

The Holy Spirit was active in the guidance of God's message to man.
(2 Samuel 23:2, 2 Peter 1:21)

### D. Service
He enabled _____.
(Exodus 31:3-5)

He enabled _____.

    Genesis 41:38    _____
    Numbers 11:16-17    _____
    Deuteronomy 34:9    _____
    Judges 3:9-10, 6:24, 11:29    _____
    1 Samuel 10:10 (c.f. 9:22), 16:13    _____

Thus, in the Old Testament economy, there are similarities to the Spirit's ministry in the New Testament.

> He is still active in bringing forth life.
>
> He still ministers or "provides gifts" to those serving and leading.
>
> The same Spirit that guided the writers of the Old Testament also guided the New Testament writers.
>
> The Holy Spirit convicts of sin.

The primary distinction of the ministry of the Spirit in the two Testaments is that the Spirit was not universal in ministry to all believers and that His abiding service could be temporary. Indwelling and sanctification were also exclusively New Testament ministries.

## II. THE MINISTRY OF THE SPIRIT IN THE LIFE OF CHRIST

### A. Prior to the _____

The ministry of the Holy Spirit in the life of Christ was prophesied in the Old Testament.
(Isaiah 11:1-3, c.f. John 3:34; Luke 4:18-21)

### B. At His _____

The Spirit was the involved in Christ's conception.
(Matthew 1:20, Luke 1:35)

### C. During His _____

| | |
|---|---|
| Anointed (Luke 4:18) | Filled (Luke 4:1) |
| Sealed (John 6:27) | Led (Luke 4:1, John 8:29) |
| Rejoiced (Luke 10:21) | Empowered (Matthew 12:28, Luke 4:1-4) |

**NOTE:** While Christ was indeed God, by the process of the incarnation, He humbled Himself and willingly surrendered the use of His divine attributes and placed Himself into the care of the Father and the Spirit in order to become our Savior and sympathetic High Priest.

**D. At His _____**

The Spirit was the personal agent involved in the death of Christ.
(Hebrews 9:14)

**E. In the _____**

The _____ and the Resurrection
(Romans 8:11)

The _____ and the Resurrection
(John 2:19-21)

The _____ and the Resurrection
(1 Peter 3:18)

## III. THE MINISTRY OF THE SPIRIT IN THE FUTURE

### A. The Spirit and the Tribulation

It is important to realize that the restraining and convicting work of the Spirit will be removed during this time only in the sense that the spiritual body of Christ (i.e. the Church) has its presence and influence removed (2 Thessalonians 2:6-8).

### B. The Spirit and the Millennium

In Relation to Believers
  The Spirit will _____ believers.
  (Ezekiel 36:25-28)

  The Spirit will _____ believers.
  (Joel 2:28-29, cf. Ezekiel 36:25-28)

In Relation to Christ
  The fullness of the Spirit will be evident in the life and ministry of the reigning Christ.
  (Isaiah 11:1-3)

## THOUGHT QUESTIONS FOR LESSON 11

1. List the similarities and differences between the ministries of the Spirit in the Old and New Testaments.

    a) Similarities

    b) Differences

2. In what way does the Church affect the ministry of the Spirit in the world? How would the removal of the Church from the world affect the ministry of the Holy Spirit?

# Lesson 12:
# The Ministry of the Holy Spirit, Part 2

This lesson will focus on the very important topic of the ministry of the Spirit in the present age and examine some of the misconceptions about the doctrine of the Holy Spirit.

## I. REGENERATION OF THE SPIRIT

This is the impartation of _____ life to those who were spiritually dead (Ephesians 2:1-2).

### A. Impartation

The regenerating work of the Spirit is accomplished in connection with the _____, the _____, and _____.
(Titus 3:2-7)

### B. Implications

Regeneration gives the believer a new _____.
(2 Corinthians 5:17)

Regeneration gives the believer _____.
(1 John 2:20)

## II. INDWELLING OF THE SPIRIT

Miraculously, the Holy Spirit dwells and abides within the body of every believer.

### A. The Possessors of the Spirit: All and Only Believers

Possession is not based on the _____.
(Acts 11:17, Romans 5:5)

Sinning Christians do possess Him.
(1 Corinthians 6:19, Ephesians 4:30)

The absence of the Holy Spirit indicates an unsaved position.
(Romans 8:9, Jude 19)

### B. The Permanence of the Spirit

A Christian cannot _____ the Spirit.
(Romans 8:9)

Sin in the Christian's life results in the _____ of the Spirit and not the departure of the Spirit.
(Ephesians 4:30).

Sin will result in the loss of fellowship with the Holy Spirit but not the loss of the indwelling of the Holy Spirit.

### C. Problems

Acts 5:32 - Has God only given the Spirit to those who obey Him?

1 Samuel 16:13-14 - Did not Saul lose the Spirit?

## III. FILLING OF THE SPIRIT

This is the ministry of the Spirit in the believer's life whereby He _____ them. To be Spirit-filled is to be Spirit-controlled.

### A. The Comparison
(Ephesians 5:18)

### B. The Command - "Be filled."
(Ephesians 5:18)

It is a _____.
(Imperative Verb)

It is _____.
(Present Verb)

### C. The Condition

Do not _____.
(1 Thessalonians 5:19)

Do not _____.
(Ephesians 4:30)

Walk in _____ to and _____ upon the Spirit of God.
(Galatians 5:16)

### D. The Consequences/Benefits

Fruit of the Spirit
(Galatians 5:22-23)

Worship
(Ephesians 5:18-20)

Submission
(Ephesians 5:21)

Proper Relationships
(Ephesians 5:22-6:9)

Service
(Acts 4:31)

# IV. BAPTISM OF THE SPIRIT

This is the act of the Holy Spirit placing the one believing into the spiritual body of Christ.

### A. Particulars

This ministry limited to the _____ Age.
(1 Corinthians 12:13)

This ministry experienced by _____ believers.
(1 Corinthians 12:13)

This ministry is experienced by believers only _____.
(Ephesians 4:5, 1 Corinthians 12:13)

Baptism is _____ commanded.

Baptism is received at _____.
(Galatians 3:3, Romans 6:3-4)

### B. Profit

Becoming members of the _____ of Christ
(1 Corinthians 12:13)

Having union with Christ in death to sin and resurrection to life
(Romans 6:1-10)

The filling with Holy Spirit is made possible.

## C. Pictures

Water Baptism          Church Membership (?)

## D. Problem - Is baptism after salvation?

Baptism, mentioned in the book of Acts only a few times, happens apparently at salvation. This was a new extension of the ministry of the Church.
(Acts 2, 10, 19)

The norm for Christians after this initial transition from the Old Covenant to the New was spiritual baptism at the time of salvation.
(1 Corinthians 12:13, Ephesians 4:5)

| BAPTISM | FILLING |
|---|---|
| Occurs only once | A continuous action |
| Not commanded | Commanded of all believers |
| Happens at salvation | Happens after salvation |
| A work of God alone | A work of God + obedience |

# V. SEALING OF THE SPIRIT

This is the work of the Spirit that guarantees the security of our salvation. It is an expression of ownership and authority.

A. _____ does the sealing.
   (2 Corinthians 1:21-22)

B. The _____ is the seal.
   (Ephesians 1:13)

C. The recipients are _____.
   (Ephesians 1:13)

D. The time is at _____.
   (Ephesians 1:13)

**NOTE:** In this verse, the tenses of the verbs indicate that hearing, believing, and sealing all occur at the same time.

## VI. GIFTS OF THE SPIRIT

This is the ministry of the Holy Spirit supplying the church with all it needs for the furtherance of the work of Christ. There are basically two kinds of gifts.

These gifts are sovereignly distributed by the Spirit (1 Corinthians 12:11), and some are given to every believer (1 Corinthians 12:1).

### A. Sign Gifts

Purpose
To _____ the _____

To _____ the _____

Catalog

Prophecy
(1 Corinthians 13:8)

Working of miracles
(1 Corinthians 12:10)

Tongues
(1 Corinthians 13:8)

Interpretation
(1 Corinthians 12:10)

Word of knowledge
(1 Corinthians 12:8)

Word of wisdom
(1 Corinthians 12:8)

Healing
(1 Corinthians 12:9)

### B. Serving Gifts
(1 Corinthians 12:28, Romans 12:5-7)

The purpose of serving gifts is to equip the local churches with the essentials for Christian ministry.

<u>Prophecy</u>: This word has the idea of forth-telling the word of God, whether it is Scripture already revealed or details of future revelation. Since we now have a complete revelation, this gift is connected with being able to stand before various groups of people and communicating to them with supernatural efficacy.

<u>Ministry</u>: This gift is the ability to do behind-the-scenes functions without the desire of leadership. It is associated with the office of deacon (same word used here).

Teaching: Teaching is the ability to present in a clear fashion the meaning of the Word of God. While this gift is required for a pastor, pastors are not the only ones who may have this gift.

Exhortation: This gift is the ability to confront with truth those who need confronting. This may also include giving direction.

Giving: This is the ability to give to the ministry of the church or those in need. It is not dependent upon the wealth of the individual but the heart which is surrendered to the Lord.

Ruling: This is the ability to direct ministry in the church by gently leading other Christians in some capacity. This gift is connected with the office of pastor, but it is not exclusively given to pastors.

Mercy: This is the ability to forgive and express the same type of mercy that our Lord does.

## C. Discerning Our Spiritual Gifts

Here are some guidelines for realizing and then utilizing your spiritual gifts:

Read the list of serving gifts. Prayerfully analyze which activity is the easiest for you.

Ask godly Christians what they think your gifts are.

Once you have an idea, ask the leadership of the church how you may utilize your gifts.

Study the biblical principles for guidelines for your gifts.

As you utilize your gifts in the church, ask people to evaluate the fruitfulness of them. This is another way to confirm what your gifts are.

## THOUGHT QUESTIONS FOR LESSON 12

1. An individual tells you that they are saved but have not received the baptism of the Spirit. How would you help this confused brother?

2. A young believer tells you she is struggling with the assurance of her salvation. What ministry of the Spirit may be of some comfort to her?

3. A believing friend shares with you that he is not that important to the church because he cannot do certain things. What might you want to share with this person that will encourage him in the faith?

4. Examine the serving gifts the Spirit has given to the church. Since all believers have been given one or some for service in the body, which one(s) do you think you possess? How could you use it/them?

# Lesson 13:
# Understanding Biblical Tongues

What exactly is the gift of tongues? Is this gift exercised today? This study will address the confusion surrounding these questions by examining the meaning and purpose of this gift.

## I. THE MEANING OF TONGUES

### A. The Scriptures

Mark 16:17
One sign which would follow (i.e. accompany) the apostles was an ability to speak in _____.

> *Kainos* means "new to the one speaking." It does connote that something had just been created.

> *Glossa* means "a human language." This is the normal use of this word in the Bible. See Acts 2:1-11 and Revelation 5:9, 7:9.

Acts 2:4
The disciples were filled with the Holy Spirit and spoke with_____ tongues.

> *Heteros* means "different" in the sense of "another kind." The disciples spoke in another known human language different from their native language. Compare verses 4 and 11 with verses 6 and 8).

> *Dialektos* means "the dialect of a nation or region."

1 Corinthians 14:2
"Unknown" in the King James Version is absent from the Greek text, as is indicated by the use of italics. Most newer translations (i.e. NASB and the NIV) correctly omit the word "unknown."

### B. The Significance

Tongues as spoken in the Bible were known, intelligible, and contemporary languages that were clearly understood by the natives of the nation or region which spoke that language, but the languages were unknown to the one who had received the gift of tongues.

www.StrivingForEternity.org

## II. THE PURPOSE OF TONGUES

### A. Tongues were used to benefit fellow believers.

In 1 Corinthians 12-14, tongues are listed and explained as gifts (see 12:4). Spiritual gifts are "favors bestowed by God, freely and graciously given."

12:7 - Spiritual gifts are given to every Christian to profit _____ (NASB: "for the common good").

12:11 - The Spirit works all spiritual gifts ("these things" refers to the gifts of vv. 8-10), distributing them as He _____

13:1-7 - The proper motive for tongues is _____.

Notice in 13:1-3 that the possession and use of spiritual gifts without love is _____ and _____

Notice in 13:5 that love does not _____ its own good.

14:12 - Those who desire spiritual gifts should seek them for the _____ of the church.

Edification is the spiritual building up or strengthening of another.

14:6 - In this verse are listed four circumstances under which the gift of tongues will benefit another believer, thereby being used according to one of its biblical purposes.

_____
_____
_____
_____

When tongues were spoken and interpreted, the content profited others because it contained direct revelation from God at a time when there was no compiled Bible. Tongues with interpretation was *one* means God used to communicate to believers *before* believers had the full written revelation associated with the life, death, resurrection, and coming of Jesus Christ.

### B. Tongues were used to convince unbelievers of…

The truth of the message.

As we discussed earlier, one of the signs which was to accompany the apostles as they went into the world preaching was tongues (Mark 16:17). A sign is a mark or token (usually a miracle) by which anything is known or distinguished.

School of Systematic Theology                                              Page | 65

As the apostles went forth preaching, the Lord _____ the proclamation with signs (Mark 16:20).

These two verses teach that the reason the apostles were given signs (including tongues) was to confirm the words which were preached. Signs were used by God to prove that the message spoken by the messengers had come from Him.

Judgment for rejecting the Gospel.

Note in 1 Corinthians 14:22 that tongues were for a _____, not for _____ but for _____.

In the context, it appears tongues were a special sign to unbelievers, especially Jews. Verse 21 is a quote from Isaiah 28:11-12, a warning that judgment would come upon the unbelieving Jews for their rejection of God's message by means of the invading army of Assyrians, who spoke a language unfamiliar to them.

Just as the tongues of Assyrians were a sign of judgment to unbelieving Jews, so the tongues of believers are a sign of judgment to unbelievers in Paul's day.

## III. THE DURATION OF TONGUES

In this section, it will be shown that the gift of tongues, like other revelatory and sign gifts, ceased when its purpose was served and was no longer needed.

### A. The Statement of Cessation

In 1 Corinthians 13:8, the Bible clearly states that tongues, along with the other two revelatory gifts of prophecy and knowledge (gifts which God used to communicate to believers in the infancy of the church), would _____ (stop).

### B. The Reason for Cessation

First Corinthians 13:9 says, "we _____ in part and _____ in part." Each time these gifts were manifested, they supplied a small part of what was to become God's completed revelation. They ceased when there was no longer a need for the partial revelation they supplied.

www.StrivingForEternity.org

## C. The Time of Cessation

First Corinthians 13:10 tells us that tongues will cease when "that which is _____ is come."

"Perfect" literally means "complete, mature." Within this context, which deals with the partial knowledge manifested by the revelatory gifts of knowledge, tongues, and prophecy, the "perfect" must refer to the completed revelation of God, which we now possess in the Bible.

## D. The Illustrations of Cessation
(1 Corinthians 13:11-12)

The Illustration of _____

> When Paul became a man, he did away with "_____" (v.11). Just as childish behavior should no longer be present in adult life, so tongues is no longer present in the "adult" (mature) life of the church. There is no more need for revelatory or sign gifts because we possess the completed revelation of God.

The Illustration of a _____

> The second illustration, which we find in verse 12, compares the quality of revelation before and after the completed revelation of God.

> "Now" (that is, at the present moment Paul was writing, approximately AD 55) Paul and other Christians saw in a mirror "dimly." In development of the metaphor, Paul next speaks of "then" (when God's revelation would be complete, as it is now), which would be more comparable to a better, face-to-face encounter.

> Before a completed Bible, God's revelation to His church was partial and, in that sense, not complete. When God's revelation was complete, Christians were able to see the totality of God's communication to man.

The Illustration of _____

> Before the completion of God's revelation, Paul knew "in part" (that is, not completely since the revelatory gifts provided only partial knowledge). After completion, he would "know even as he is known." In other words, he would know fully and clearly all of God's revelation in the same full and clear way that he has been known by God.

## THOUGHT QUESTIONS FOR LESSON 13

1. How do you think a Christian receives the gift of tongues?

2. Is a believer to pray in tongues? Why or why not?

3. Today, the gift of tongues is for…
   a) all believers.
   b) most believers.
   c) some believers.
   d) none of the above

4. Is there a purpose for speaking tongues in the church? If so, what is the purpose?

5. The gift of tongues in the Bible is…
   a) an angelic language.
   b) a known language unknown to the speaker.
   c) a totally unique language unknown to the speaker.

6. Circle one: the gift of tongues was ( VERY / SOMEWHAT / NOT VERY ) important in the early church.

# SECTION IV:

# The Doctrine of Angels

# Lesson 14:
# Holy and Evil Angels

The doctrine of angels is very interesting yet frequently misunderstood. Some believe angels are humans in the after-life. Others have either exaggerated or ignored what Scripture teaches about angels. The Bible does devote a good portion of revelation about angels. Seventeen Old Testament books and 17 New Testament books mention angels. There are 108 Old Testament and 165 New Testament verses that discuss angels.

We will examine the biblical data available to help us understand who angels are, from where they came, and what their ministries are.

## I. THE CREATION OF ANGELS
(Psalm 148:2-5, Colossians 1:16)

### A. The Time of Their Creation

While we do not have specific revelation about the creation of angels, we still see that angels were created at some time _____ the creation for two main reasons.

They were _____ while observing Creation.
(Job 38:6-7)

Satan (who was an angel) must have been created prior to Genesis _____.

### B. The Nature of Angels at Creation

They are _____.
(Hebrews 1:14)

Each angel was _____ created by God.
(Matthew 22:28-30)

They are _____ from both man and God and will be for all eternity.
(Hebrews 2:6-8; 12:22-24)

They have _____.
> Intellect  
> (1 Peter 1:12, Matthew 28:5)
>
> Emotion  
> (Job 38:7, Luke 15:10)
>
> Will  
> (Jude 6, Isaiah 14:12-15)

Their power and abilities are _____.

> They are limited by _____.  
> (Ephesians 1:20-21)
>
> They are more powerful than _____, but their power, knowledge, and presence are limited.  
> (2 Peter 2:11)
>
> Angels are not to be _____.  
> (Colossians 2:18)

They are _____ beings, but they are not _____.  
(Luke 20:36)

Their abode is in _____ while still having _____ to the earth.  
(Mark 13:32, Daniel 9:20-23)

## II. THE HOLY ANGELS

### A. Their Organization

The _____ of their organization is seen in Colossians 1:16 and Ephesians 1:21.

Their number is said to be _____.  
(Hebrews 12:22, Daniel 7:10)

Another indication of organization is the mention of an _____ His name is Michael.  
(1 Thessalonians 4:16, Jude 9)

We see the Archangel _____ other angels.  
(Revelation 12:7)

## B. Their Designations

### General Names

| Sons of God | Morning stars | God's host |
|---|---|---|
| (Job 1:6, 38:7) | (Job 38:7) | (Genesis 32:1-2) |
| Sons of the Mighty | Holy ones | Watchers |
| (Psalm 89:6) | (Psalm 89:7) | (Daniel 4:13, 17) |
| Hosts of heaven | Ministering spirits | |
| (Luke 2:13) | (Hebrews 1:14) | |

### Specific Names

| Michael | Gabriel |
|---|---|
| (Daniel 12:1) | (Daniel 9:21, Luke 1:26) |
| Seraphim | Cherubim |
| (Isaiah 6:2, 6) | (Genesis 3:24, Ezekiel 10:1-20) |
| Living creatures | Angel of water |
| (Revelation 4:6) | (Revelation 16:5) |
| Angel of the abyss | Angel of fire |
| (Revelation 9:11) | (Revelation 14:8) |

## C. Their Ministries

Their ministry in connection with _____

| Praise | Worship |
|---|---|
| (Job 38:7, Psalm 103:20) | (Isaiah 6:2-3) |

Service
(Genesis 19:12-13; Revelation 19:10, 22:8-9)

Their ministry in connection with _____

We see angels _____ the birth of Christ.
(Luke 1:26-33)

After the temptation of Christ, angels _____ Him.
(Matthew 4:11)

During His prayer in Gethsemane just prior to His crucifixion, they _____ to Him.
(Luke 22:43)

Angels _____ His resurrection.
(Matthew 28:6)

Angels also were present at the _____ of Christ.
(Acts 1:10)

In the future, all angels will be present both at the _____
(1 Thessalonians 4:16) and the _____ of Christ.
(Matthew 25:31)

Their ministry in connection with _____

Angels have the general ministry of _____ believers.
(Hebrews 1:14)

Angels seem to be involved in the _____ of _____.
(Acts 12:7, Revelation 5:8)

They observe Christian's and their _____.
(1 Timothy 5:21; 1 Corinthians 4:9; 11:10; 1 Peter 1:12)

Angels rejoice in the evangelistic efforts of Christians.
(Luke 15:10)

Angels seem to have a ministry to the righteous at _____.
(Luke 16:22, Jude 9)

Angels were active in the giving of _____.
(Acts 7:53, Hebrews 2:2, Galatians 3:19)

Their Ministry in Connection with _____

Michael seemed to have a special relationship to Israel.
(Daniel 10:21, 12:1)

Angels will be active in gathering elect Israel in the Millennium.
(Matthew 24:31)

Their ministry in connection with _____

Angels will be involved with the future _____ of God. (Revelation 8-10)

Angels will act as reapers at the end of the age.
(Matthew 13:39, 49, 50; 25:31-33)

## III. THE FALLEN ANGELS

### A. Their Demise

They apparently fell at the same time as _____.
All angels who did not fall were confirmed in _____.

### B. Their Description

They are spirit beings.  They are intelligent beings.
(Matthew 17:18, Mark 9:25)  (Mark 1:24, Matthew 8:29)

### C. Their Devices

They are _____ of Satan.
(Ephesians 6:11-12, Matthew 12:26-27)

While attempting to thwart the plans of God (Daniel 10:10-14, Revelation 16:13-16), they actually execute it:

In the discipline of believers  In trials
(1 Corinthians 5:5)  (the story of Job)

In the cultivation of dependence  In the punishment of the ungodly
(2 Corinthians 12:7-9)  (Psalm 78:49)

They may _____ unsaved men.
(Matthew 4:24)

They generate _____.
(1 Corinthians 10:18-20)

They disperse _____.
(1 Timothy 4:1)

### D. Their Destiny
(Matthew 25:41, Revelation 20:10)

## THOUGHT QUESTIONS FOR LESSON 14

1. A Jehovah's Witness tells you that Jesus Christ in His preincarnate state was Michael the Archangel. How would you answer this person?

2. You and your child are watching a television show in which angels are depicted as souls of departed men. How would you help your child with this misunderstanding?

3. Compare Luke 15:10 with 1 Peter 1:12. From these two Scriptures, what truths can we glean about angels and their part in salvation?

4. Comparing all the ministries of angels, what three activities describe their overall purpose in relation to mankind?

    1)

    2)

    3)

# Lesson 15:
# Satan

An understanding of the doctrine of angels must also include a study of Satan. Keep in mind that the creation and nature of angels studied in the previous lesson are also true of our adversary.

## I. DESCRIPTION OF SATAN

### A. His Origin
(Ezekiel 28:11-17, Isaiah 14:12-14)

At his creation, he possessed (Ezekiel 28:12):

_____.
_____.
_____.

He dwelt in the _____ of God.
(Ezekiel 28:13)

He was _____ to God.
(Ezekiel 28:13)

His fall was a result of his _____.
(Ezekiel 28:17, Isaiah 14:12-14, 1 Timothy 3:6).

### B. His Personality

Satan _____ all the elements of personality.
    Intellect
    (2 Corinthians 2:11, Matthew 4:6, Ephesians 6:11)

    Will
    (2 Timothy 2:26, Isaiah 14:12-13)

    Emotions
    (Luke 22:31, 1 Timothy 3:6, Revelation 12:12)

Satan _____ all the actions of personality.
    Speaks
    (Job 1:9, Matthew 4:1-11)

Accuses
(Job 1:9-10, Revelation 12:10)

Tempts
(Matthew 4:3)

## C. His Character

He is a _____.
(John 8:44)

He is a _____.
(John 8:44)

He is a _____.
(1 John 3:8)

# II. DESIGNATIONS OF SATAN

## A. Satan

This name characterizes Satan as _____ or the _____. This name is used 52 times in the Old Testament.
(Zechariah 3:1; Matthew 4:10; Revelation 12:9, 20:2)

## B. Devil

This designation emphasizes Satan's work of _____ and reveals that Satan accuses believers before God.
(Matthew 4:1; Ephesians 4:27; Revelation 12:9, 20:2; Job 1-2)

## C. Lucifer

It means _____ and indicates his _____ (beauty).
(Isaiah 14:12)

## D. Beelzebub

Also "lord of the flies," this term is used by the Jews as a _____ of Satan.
(Matthew 10:25, 12:24)

### E. Serpent

This designation of Satan connected to him in the Old Testament and applied to him in the New Testament emphasizes his_____.
(Genesis 3:1, 2 Corinthians 11:3, Revelation 12:9)

### F. Belial

The title means _____.
(2 Corinthians 6:15)

### G. Abaddon (Apollyon)

Both names for Satan identify him as a _____.
(Revelation 9:11)

### H. Tempter

We see him fulfill this role in the life of men as well as in Christ's.
(Matthew 4:1-11, 1 Thessalonians 3:5)

### I. Prince of this World

This title and those related to it (i.e. god of this world, prince of the power of the air) identify Satan's controlling influence on our _____.
(Ephesians 2:2, 2 Corinthians 4:4, John 12:31)

## III. DOMINION OF SATAN

**A. He is the ruler of _____.**
(Matthew 25:41)

**B. He is the ruler of _____.**
(John 12:31, Ephesians 2:2)

## IV. DOMAIN OF SATAN

**A. He is _____ in the heavenlies.**
(Ephesians 6:11-12)

**B. He has _____ to heaven.**
   (Revelation 12:10, Job 1:6)

**C. He is _____ on Earth.**
   (1 Peter 5:8, Matthew 13:38-39)

## V. DEVICES OF SATAN

**A. In Relation to _____**

   Counterfeit
      False _____
      (2 Corinthians 11:13-15)

      False _____
      (Galatians 1:6-9)

      False _____
      (1 Timothy 4:1-3)

      False _____
      (1 John 2:18, 22; 4:3)

      False _____
      (Matthew 13:38-39)

      False _____
      (Matthew 24:24; Revelation 13:3, 12-15)

   Rebellion
   (2 Thessalonians 2:3-11, Revelation 13:1-18)

   Limited
      He is limited by _____.
      (Job 1:12, 2:6; 1 John 5:18)

      His _____ was promised by God and provided at the cross.
      (Genesis 3:14-15, John 12:31)

   Judged
      Cast from _____ position
      (Ezekiel 28:16)

Cast out of heaven in the _____
(Revelation 20:13)

Confined at beginning of the _____
(Revelation 20:2)

Cast into _____ at the end of the Millennium
(Revelation 20:10)

## B. In Relation to _____

Their conflict was _____.
(Genesis 3:15)

He _____ Christ.
(Matthew 4:1)

He _____ Judas to betray Christ.
(John 13:27)

## C. In Relation to _____

He is instrumental in their _____.
(Revelation 20:3)

He is instrumental in their _____.
(Revelation 16:13-16)

## D. In Relation to _____

He slanders and accuses.
(Revelation 12:10)

He hinders service.
(1 Thessalonians 2:18)

He attempts to thwart the efforts of evangelism.
(Matthew 13:19)

He tempts to sin.
(Acts 5:3, 1 Corinthians 7:5, 1 Timothy 1:6)

He incites persecution.
(Revelation 2:10)

He infiltrates the church with false _____ and false _____.
(2 Peter 2:1-19, Jude 4)

## VI. DEFENSE AGAINST SATAN

**A. Salvation**
(Ephesians 2:1-9)

**B. Vigilance**
(2 Corinthians 2:11, 1 Peter 5:8)

**C. Submission**
(James 4:7)

**D. Armor**
(Ephesians 6:10-18)

## THOUGHT QUESTIONS FOR LESSON 15

1. Read 1 Peter 5:8. What picture do you see concerning Satan's desire for each believer?

2. Satan's names and titles indicate one or some of his attributes. List the applicable attributes of each. Then, record how each may affect a believer.

    A. Satan -

    B. Devil -

    C. Lucifer -

    D. Serpent -

    E. Belial -

    F. Abaddon (Apollyon) -

    G. Tempter -

    H. Prince of this world -

3. Read 1 Timothy 4:1. What is the source of false doctrine and false teachers?

4. Read Ephesians 6:10-18. List the weapons and protection in our battle with Satan's forces.

# BIBLIOGRAPHY

Boice, James M. *Foundations of the Christian Faith*. Downers Grove, Ill.: InterVarsity Press, 1986.

Bookman, Douglas. Unpublished Class Notes on Theology Proper. Minnesota: Pillsbury Baptist Bible College, 1983.

Bubeck, Mark I. *The Adversary*. Chicago: Moody Press, 1975.

Chafer, Lewis Sperry. *Grace: The Glorious Theme*. Grand Rapids: Zondervan Publishing, 1950.

Chafer, Lewis Sperry. *Satan: His Motive and Methods*. Grand Rapids: Zondervan Publishers, 1964.

Charnock, Stephen. *The Existence and Attributes of God*. Grand Rapids: Baker Book House, 1979.

Culver, Robert Duncan. *The Life of Christ*. Grand Rapids: Baker Book House, 1976.

Dickason, C. Fred. *Angels: Elect and Evil*. Chicago: Moody Press, 1975.

Gromacki, Robert. *The Virgin Birth: Doctrine of Deity*. New York: Thomas Nelson Publishers, 1974.

Hocking, David. *The Nature of God in Plain Language*. Waco, Texas: Word Book Publishers, 1984.

Kaiser, Christopher B. *The Doctrine of God*. Westchester, Ill.: Crossway Books, 1982.

Lawlor, George L. <u>Almah</u> ...*Virgin or Young Woman*. Des Plaines, Ill.: Regular Baptist Press, 1973.

Lightner, Robert P. *The God of the Bible*. Grand Rapids: Baker Book House, 1973.

MacArthur, John. *God, Satan, and Angels*. Panorama City, CA: Word of Grace Communication, 1989.

Machen, J. Gresham. *The Virgin Birth of Christ*. Grand Rapids: Baker Book House, 1982.

Mueller, Marc. Unpublished Class Notes on Theology Proper. Sun Valley, CA.: The Master's Seminary, 1988.

Packer, J.I. *Knowing God*. Downers Grove, Ill.: InterVarsity Press, 1973.

Pentecost, J. Dwight. *Your Adversary the Devil*. Grand Rapids: Zondervan Publishers, 1969.

Ryrie, Charles. *Basic Theology*. Wheaton, Ill.: Victor Books, 1987.

Ryrie, Charles. *The Holy Spirit*. Chicago: Moody Press, 1965.

Stone, Nathan. *Names of God*. Chicago: Moody Press, 1944.

Tozer, A.W. *The Knowledge of the Holy*. New York: Harper and Row Publishers, 1961.

Unger, Merrill F. *The Baptism and Gifts of the Holy Spirit*. Chicago: Moody Press, 1974.

Walvoord, John F. *Jesus Christ Our Lord*. Chicago: Moody Press, 1969.

Walvoord, John F. *The Holy Spirit*. Grand Rapids: Zondervan Publishers, 1958.

www.ingramcontent.com/pod-product-compliance
Lightning Source LLC
Chambersburg PA
CBHW081205170426
43197CB00018B/2932